INCREDIBLE ICE

Scott Wilken

Big Buddy Books

An Imprint of Abdo Publishing
abdobooks.com

abdobooks.com

Published by Abdo Publishing, a division of ABDO, PO Box 398166, Minneapolis, Minnesota 55439.

Printed in the United States of America, North Mankato, Minnesota
052025
092025

Design: Elena Klinkner, Mighty Media, Inc.
Production: Mighty Media, Inc.
Editor: Ruthie Van Oosbree
Cover Photograph: Parilov/Shutterstock
Interior Photographs: aceshot1/Shutterstock, p. 24; BillionPhotos.com/Adobe Stock, p. 28 (salt); an ma/Shutterstock, pp. 6–7; Andreas_Bergerstedt/Shutterstock, p. 17; BillionPhotos.com/Adobe Stock, p. 28 (ice); grey/Adobe Stock, p. 28 (can); Harris and Ewing, National Bureau of Standards, courtesy AIP Emilio Segrè Visual Archives/Wikimedia Commons, p. 13; Jared Stanley/Wikimedia Commons, pp. 26–27; Jo Ann Snover/iStockphoto, pp. 18–19; jollyphoto/Shutterstock, p. 10; Kathy Clark/Shutterstock, pp. 14–15; K8Y/Shutterstock, p. 9; Linda Cook/Adobe Stock, p. 28 (paper and scissors); Maria Moroz/Shutterstock, pp. 22–23; Markus Semmler/Adobe Stock, p. 21 (hair ice); Michele/Adobe Stock, p. 28 (marker); Mighty Media, Inc., p. 29; Olga Gavrilova/Shutterstock, p. 5; Sanit/Adobe Stock, p. 28 (spoon); vadarshop/Adobe Stock, p. 28 (tablespoon); Wikimedia Commons, p. 21 (Alfred Wegener)
Design Elements: Mighty Media, Inc.

Library of Congress Control Number: 2024948579

Publisher's Cataloging-in-Publication Data
Names: Wilken, Scott, author.
Title: Incredible ice / by Scott Wilken
Description: Minneapolis, Minnesota : Abdo Publishing, 2026 | Series: Weather wonders | Includes online resources and index.
Identifiers: ISBN 9781098296377 (lib. bdg.) | ISBN 9798384917809 (ebook)
Subjects: LCSH: Ice--Juvenile literature. | Storms--Juvenile literature. | Weather--Juvenile literature. | Sky--Juvenile literature. | Cold weather conditions--Juvenile literature.
Classification: DDC 551.6--dc23

Contents

Icy Conditions

Snow and ice may be unwelcome. They make roads and sidewalks slippery. It can be dangerous to drive and walk on them. But if the conditions are just right, snow and ice can be very beautiful.

Icicles are just one of the many beautiful forms ice can take.

Three rare but beautiful ice and snow **formations** are frost flowers, hair ice, and snow rollers. They all need very special weather and environments to form. Frost flowers and hair ice form on certain plants. Snow rollers form on windy winter days.

You have to be in the right place at the right time to see hair ice.

Frost Flowers

Frost flowers look like ribbons or flower petals made of ice. They form on the stems of some plants. Only about 40 plants are known to produce frost flowers. They are all **herbaceous** plants.

Frost flowers are also called ice fringes, ice filaments, rabbit ice, and ice flowers.

Frost flowers are often seen in late fall when the air temperature first drops below freezing.

Frost flowers occur when the air is freezing cold but the ground has not frozen yet. Moisture from the soil and sap travels up the stem. The moisture pushes out through cracks in the stem. The cold air freezes it into ice. More moisture pushes out and freezes, adding to the ice layer.

Learning About Frost Flowers

English scientist John Herschel was one of the first people to study frost flowers. His description and illustrations were **published** in 1833. In 1892, American scientist William Hamilton Gibson noticed that frost flowers required moisture from the soil, not just from the plant's sap.

In 1914, American scientist William Coblentz found that roots weren't necessary to form frost flowers.

Scientists today still don't know everything about frost flowers. But they are able to create the conditions to grow them. People can see and learn about frost flowers at places such as **arboretums** and nature **preserves**.

Scientist Bob Harms named frost flowers *crystallofolia*, which is Latin for "ice leaves."

Hair Ice

Hair ice looks like soft **strands** of white hair. It forms on rotting wood from certain types of trees, such as maple and oak trees. Hair ice needs moist air, just the right temperature, and a special **fungus** in order to form. It also only occurs at a certain **latitude**.

The fungus that causes hair ice is called *Exidiopsis effusa*.

For hair ice to form, the air temperature needs to be just below freezing. But the rotting wood can't be frozen. Moisture in the air starts to freeze on the wood's surface. Then the **fungus** releases **chemicals** that cause the ice to grow in long **strands**.

Hair ice strands are about 0.01 millimeters thick.

Hair Ice Studies

German scientist Alfred Wegener wrote about hair ice in 1918. He saw a **fungus** on the wood where hair ice grew. He thought this fungus may be important to the growth of hair ice. In 2015, a team of scientists **identified** the fungus and proved that Wegener was right.

Wegener is also famous for his idea that land masses move around Earth.

Snow Rollers

Snow rollers look like powdered doughnuts on a snowy field. For snow rollers to form, the temperature must be slightly above 32 degrees Fahrenheit (0°C). There must be a thin layer of new snow. And the wind must be blowing at about 30 miles per hour (48 kmh).

Snow rollers are also called snow bales, wind snowballs, and snow doughnuts.

Snow rollers can be more than 18 inches (46 cm) tall.

Snow rollers form in open areas without many trees or plants. The old snow must be icy or crusty so the new snow doesn't stick to it. Then, the wind makes the new snow curl up and roll across the ground. As the snow rolls, it picks up more snow and gets bigger. It rolls until it becomes too heavy for the wind to move it.

Wondrous Weather

Frost flowers, hair ice, and snow rollers are true winter weather wonders. But not all snow and ice **formations** are so unusual. Common winter sights such as snow drifts and icicles can also be beautiful. What is your favorite snow or ice formation?

Needle ice grows when moisture moves upward in soil, then freezes.

Create a Frosty Friend!

What You Need

- aluminum can
- permanent markers
- paper
- scissors
- tape
- ice
- 3 tablespoons (15 mL) salt
- spoon

What You Do

1. Draw a face on the can with permanent markers. Cut ears or other parts out of paper and decorate them with marker. Tape them to the can. You might create a polar bear, arctic fox, snowy owl, or any other white creature!
2. Fill the can to the top with ice and add salt. Stir. Add more ice if needed to reach the top. Stir again.

3. Let the can sit until it frosts over! Add more ice and salt if needed. The salt makes the mixture colder than ice alone. It is below the freezing point of water. Moisture from the air collects on the outside of the cold can and freezes.

Glossary

arboretum—a garden where trees and other plants are grown for people to study and enjoy.

chemical (KEH-mih-kuhl)—something that can cause reactions and changes.

formation—something that has been formed into a certain shape.

fungus—a type of living thing that usually produces spores, such as mold, yeast, and mushrooms.

herbaceous—a type of plant that is green or bendy but not woody.

identify—to find out what something is.

latitude—a measure of distance north and south from Earth's equator. On a map, latitude lines run in the same direction as the equator.

preserve—an area set aside to keep plants and animals safe.

publish—to print the work of an author.

strand—a long, thin piece of something, such as hair or thread.

Online Resources

To learn more about ice formations, please visit **abdobooklinks.com** or scan this QR code. These links are routinely monitored and updated to provide the most current information available.

Index